LANDSCAPE of CONFLICT
Israel's Northern Frontier

Photographs and Narrative
Arieh Larkey

gefen גפן
publishing house בית הוצאה לאור
JERUSALEM ◆ NEW YORK

Cover Design & Layout: Arieh Larkey

1 3 5 7 9 8 6 4 2

Gefen Publishing House
POB 36004, Jerusalem 91360, Israel
972-2-538-0247 • orders@gefenpublishing.com

Gefen Books
12 New Street Hewlett, NY 11557, USA
516-295-2805 • gefenny@gefenpublishing.com

www.israelbooks.com

Printed in Israel   *Send for our free catalogue*

ISBN 965-229-305-9

PUBLISHER'S FORWARD

As one of our prominent authors, Mr. Larkey visits our Jerusalem offices on a regular basis. On one such occasion, during the publication of his second book, "Ruth – Revisited: A Survivor's Journey," he happened to bring along – just for our interest – an album of photographs he had taken during his stay on a frontier kibbutz.

Within seconds of viewing these extraordinary landscapes, I realized that I was gazing upon the genesis of another book. "These photographs have to be shared with the world," I blurted out. The astonished author concurred, and soon afterward an agreement was reached to publish them in book form.

We are pleased to present "Landscape of Conflict – Israel's Northern Frontier" as one of our foremost new publications.

Sincerely,

Dror Greenfield
Gefen Publishing House Ltd.
Jerusalem

AUTHOR / PHOTOGRAPHER'S PREFACE

Perched high on my private lookout point above Israel's northern frontier, I had an unobstructed view of the Golan Heights, Mt. Hermon and the valley and rolling hills below, which physically connect three neighboring countries into a seamless jigsaw puzzle of contention: Israel, Lebanon and Syria.

The pastoral scenes before me, belied the political and emotional upheavals which the world has focused on through television images of this embattled region of the world. My eyes and camera lens focused only on the exquisite beauty which I was privileged to gaze-upon.

Rather than trying to describe each scene or entitle each photograph, I have decided to simply share my feelings as I pressed down on the shutter; freezing my momentary glance at an extraordinarily beautiful landscape, but one which is also fraught with uncertainty and conflict in the near and distant future.

DEDICATION

This book is dedicated to my grandsons Nicholas and Kyle,
with love

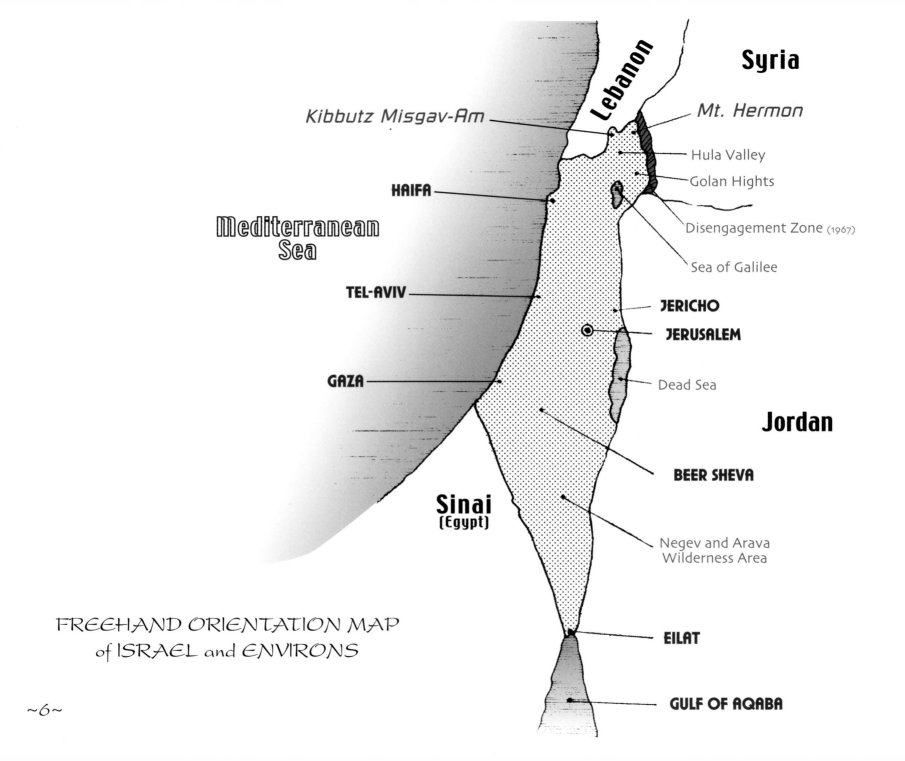

Syria

Lebanon

Kibbutz Misgav-Am

Mt. Hermon

Hula Valley

Golan Hights

HAIFA

Disengagement Zone (1967)

Mediterranean Sea

Sea of Galilee

TEL-AVIV

JERICHO

JERUSALEM

GAZA

Dead Sea

Jordan

BEER SHEVA

Sinai (Egypt)

Negev and Arava Wilderness Area

FREEHAND ORIENTATION MAP of ISRAEL and ENVIRONS

EILAT

GULF OF AQABA

KIBBUTZ MISGAV-AM

Misgav-Am was founded on November 2, 1945. Most of the original settlers came from the Palmach - a pre-state paramilitary organization preparing for independence. Once established, the kibbutz was able to receive and assimilate dozens of straggling survivors of the Holocaust, who somehow managed to find their way to Eretz Yisrael after the Allied liberation of Europe.

Members of zionist youth movements and scout organizations were also among the first settlers to establish this mountainside community in the Upper Galilee, sitting 841 meters above sea level on the north-west side of the Naftali mountain range; its western boundary congruent with the international border between Israel and Lebanon.

To the north and west lies the rugged high-country of southern Lebanon. To the east, the gently undulating Hula Valley below, once a vast mosquito infested swampland, now cradles many sister kibbutzim in its drained fertile acreage. At the eastern edge of the valley a high plateau known as the Golan Heights makes its way from the south, rising dramatically - directly opposite Misgav-Am - into a magnificent peak - Mount Hermon, over 2000 meters above sea level.

Awakening one morning before dawn, I couldn't seem to fall back to sleep. Easing myself out of bed, my body shivered as it encountered the sharp chill which had penetrated our mountain cabin in mid-winter. A strong cup of hot coffee relieved my discomfort. Even though it was bitterly cold, I stepped out – coffee in hand – onto our balcony, overlooking a valley spotted with the dazzling night-lights of three different countries. The view was mesmerizing.

As I gazed out into the night sky, a faint glimmer of light was beginning to reveal itself above our mountain – Mt. Hermon. Within seconds the light intensified and the sun rose above the horizon. A new day had dawned right before my eyes. At that very moment, all I could think about was ... why didn't I have my camera with me to record the spectacular event I had just witnessed. The next evening I intentionally set the alarm for 4:30 am - much to my wife's dismay. But she really understood.

The same early hour ... the same bitter cold ... another cup of hot coffee. But this time – I had camera in hand. My only remaining challenge was to somehow get that perfect shot; the moment when the sun just peaks itself over the horizon. My solution was simple. As soon as I saw that faint aura of light above the mountain, I'd start clicking the shutter. Twenty-four clicks later, another day had dawned. One of my shots had to have recorded that very special moment. I was right!

Everyone who knows and loves our mountain as I do, is aware of her mischievous and sometimes bashful temperament. At times, she cloaks herself in a veil of fog in order to playfully hide from her ardent admirers. She even goes so far as to blur her image with trillions of tiny specks of sand swept in by the winds of the east. But we, her faithful devotees, are patient. For we know that – upon occasion – she sheds her bashfulness and allows us to gaze in awe at her most regal beauty.

What's the connection between these two very different photographs? The one on the left seems to be an innocuous picture of loudspeakers - sitting atop a tree canopy. Why include it with such beautiful landscapes as the one shown on the right. Not all is as it seems!

Looking more closely at the tranquil landscape, we can see an innocent- looking, serpentine road meandering its way through the valley floor. The reality of that small detail is a bit more dramatic. The road is, in fact, the volatile border between two hostile nations; a great divide between peoples and their cultures. The loudspeakers are an improvised 'early warning system' for a rural mountain community.

Rolling hills of farmland. Beautiful multicolored patches of cultivated land in mid-summer. It could be a pretty landscape from anywhere in the world - except for the presence of that weathered watchtower guarding the countryside.

Somewhere in the Australian outback rises a
giant monolith known as Ayers Rock; its color –
sandy red. Our mountain seems to delight in its
many disguises and impersonations; this time, a
distant cousin from 'down under'.

All sunsets are beautiful! But every now and then, mother nature really 'struts her stuff'. And I was lucky enough to be there - camera in hand.

Following page: MORNING PANORAMA

Like sunsets, sunrises can be equally tantalizing for the photographer; the thought of capturing the glitter of night-lights still burning and yet at the same moment, the blackness of the night sky having already given way to the pastel colors of morning.

Generations of poets and writers, all have written about their feelings as the harshness of winter finally subsides and 'spring is in the air'. I was privileged to witness this delightful change of season from a unique vantage point. My photographs are my feelings.

A 'PEEK' THROUGH THE CHERRY BLOSSOMS - Every time I pass our bedroom window in the spring, my senses of sight and smell are simply overwhelmed. After several adjustments to the focus, I finally succeeded in getting the shot I wanted. A month or so later, my sense of taste was treated to the same delightful experience.

Whenever we mention fog, each of us conjures-up an image of that mysterious and, at times, dangerous ground-hugging cloud. A favorite among my own nostalgic images is from the 1940's movie "Key Largo", where Humphrey Bogart is desperately trying to guide his small fishing trawler through the fog laden Florida Keys and back to the safety of shore and the waiting arms of his new girlfriend - Lauren Bacall. Two of my *latest* favorites are shown here.

The use of words to describe this photograph...
or even my feelings as I clicked the shutter,
would be a travesty. Enjoy!

Here in the Middle East, rain isn't taken for granted. The level of the Sea of Galilee, the collecting reservoir for all the surrounding sources of our fresh water, is of daily concern. Thus, when the winter rains finally arrive in late November or even as late as mid-December, it's a time of national rejoicing. And if the cold winds are blowing in from the north, it's snow on the peaks of Mt. Hermon. What a sight to see!

And if by any stroke of luck, the temperature in the lower hills and valley happens to drop below that magical number of 0^{0} centigrade $(32^{0} F)$, then we're in for a real treat. It doesn't happen every year, but when it does, it's worth braving the cold, so as to record this occasional – but always welcome – visit by the polar winds.

THE MORNING AFTER ...

When I stepped out onto our balcony the next morning, I just had to snap a shot of the tile covered pergola which shields us from the intense sunlight during the summer months. That's our cherry tree beyond – this time its branches laden with the white fluff of snow in lieu of the blossoms of spring. Both visions are exquisite!

In order to shoot this 'expanded' view, I had to climb – very carefully – onto the roof above the pergola. The apex of the guard-rail, shown in the foreground, is the spot where most of the photographs were taken. I'm really glad I made the effort!

When I first saw this 'mirage', I wondered whether real mirages have ever been captured on film – or whether the ones we see in the movies are just trick photography. I had to get a shot of this multi-layered phenomenon before it disappeared.

When I snapped this photograph – unlike the others – I was not aware of the scene that eventually emerged on the processed film. My reaction was humbling – almost reverent.

A CLOSER LOOK ...

A beautiful canyon, carved into the landscape by one of the freshwater streams feeding the Jordan River, which eventually flows into the Sea of Galilee some 40 kilometers to the south – waters which emanate from the mountains and springs in one country, flow naturally through another and then on to another. Water – not oil – is a major source of potential conflict in our little corner of the Middle East.

'SISTERS' in the VALLEY

"... To the East, the gently undulating Hula Valley
below, once a vast mosquito-infested swampland,
now cradles many sister kibbutzim in its drained
and fertile acreage."

SEIZE THE MOMENT

It's not often that mother-nature allows us the opportunity to glance directly at the sun for more than just a fleeting moment. It happened one day - 'on my watch' - and I was lucky enough to have my camera close by.

WILL-O'-THE-WISP

This comet-like wisp of cloud simply wasn't there
when I clicked the shutter to take this photograph.
It's a mystery - but a beautiful one none the less.

author /
photographer
and his wife
Larisa
on their balcony
overlooking the
"LANDSCAP
OF CONFLIC

photo by: Michael Walter, Misgav-Am.

ABOUT THE AUTHOR/PHOTOGRAPHER

Arieh (Richard) Larkey was born in Newark, New Jersey in 1935. At eighteen he volunteered to serve in the American army and was sent to Germany as part of the NATO forces. It was there, that a heightened awareness of his Jewish roots would take hold, eventually leading – later in life – to an amazing change of direction. Larkey made aliyah in 1971.

An architectural career consumed most of Larkey's adult life, but at the age of 60 he put down his drafting tools, closed his Jerusalem office and began to write. While working on his second book, he took a year away from city life to live and write in the high country of Israel's northern frontier – on Kibbutz Misgav-Am.

The views from his balcony were so spectacular that he decided to 'snap a few shots' in order to record his year's stay on his mountain-top retreat. The resulting photographs were so astonishing that he and his publisher decided to share them.... Thus bringing about the reproduction of these amazing landscapes.

Mr. Larkey and his wife Larisa now live in the small historical village of Zichron Yaacov, in northern Israel, overlooking the Mediterranean coastline, but often return to their mountain-top retreat when the spirit moves or his muse beckons.

OTHER TITLES BY ARIEH LARKEY

A TOWNHOUSE IN JERUSALEM

Gefen Publishing House, Jerusalem, 1996

A lively memoir about the author's aliyah experiences

Hardcover, 376 pp
ISBN 965-229-153-6

RUTH - REVISITED

a survivor's journey

Gefen Publishing House, Jerusalem, 2001

An adventure / love story about a young Holocaust survivor's passages through life

Hardcover, 296 pp
ISBN 965-229-226-4